The Honourable Mercenary

The Honourable Mercenary

Centennial Millennial edition

HALFDAN OLDADSON

For scholarship and all other purposes, the authenticity of this manuscript is unconfirmed and, therefore, should be considered apocryphal.
U.S. Copyright ©2015

Originally Published by:
Faeroe Borealis Publishing

English Version Printed in the United States of America
U.S. Library of Congress No. 2015909423
CreateSpace Independent Publishing Platform
North Charleston, South Carolina

ISBN-13: 9781514282885
ISBN-10 1514282887

Illustrations by Rose Pryor, Cornwall, U.K.

Table of Contents

PAGE

I.	What, then, is honour?	1
II.	When does a mercenary know that he is suited to his profession?	1
III.	Is it possible for a Berserker to follow the path of an honourable mercenary?	2
IV.	Should a mercenary foreknow his adversary to be his equal?	3
V.	Should a mercenary fight to redeem his honour?	4
VI.	Should a mercenary boast of his battles so that he is known to the Kings?	4
VII.	Does a mercenary fight for the King or for the King's cause?	5
VIII.	Should a mercenary accept an engagement if he believes he will be defeated?	6
IX.	When must a mercenary warn off his King?	7

X.	If a King orders a mercenary to use subterfuge, what should be the mercenary's response?	7
XI.	Must a mercenary always follow the instructions of his King?	9
XII.	Why should a King hire an honourable mercenary?	11
XIII.	Does a mercenary continue to fight for a King proven to be evil?	12
XIV.	May a mercenary ever turn against his King?	12
XV.	What is a mercenary's obligation to a King for whom he has fought?	13
XVI.	What should a mercenary charge for his services?	14
XVII.	When may a mercenary agree to share in the spoils of battle?	15
XVIII.	If a King promises gold for victory but does not pay his victorious mercenary, does the mercenary collect with his saex?	16
XIX.	Should a mercenary invoke the gods against his adversary?	17
XX.	Should a mercenary break bread with his adversary?	17
XXI.	Should a mercenary discuss the upcoming battle with his adversary?	19

XXII.	Should victory be achieved through subterfuge and awful deeds if Odin favors one's cause?	19
XXIII.	Can honourable mercenaries survive if dishonourable mercenaries have an advantage in battle?	21
XXIV.	Should a mercenary taunt his adversary?	22
XXV.	How does a mercenary overcome fear?	23
XXVI.	Must a mercenary press the battle?	23
XXVII.	Should a mercenary accommodate an adversary by delaying battle?	24
XXVIII.	Is there a way to best engage a dishonourable adversary?	25
XXIX.	How does a mercenary treat the uninvolved?	25
XXX.	Are there some throats that should not feel the saex?	26
XXXI.	Is a mercenary responsible for the acts of his huscarls?	27
XXXII.	Once victorious, should a mercenary disfigure his adversary?	28
XXXIII.	If a mercenary fights for an evil King, is he more likely to die?	29
XXXIV.	When must a mercenary surrender?	29

XXXV.	Should a mercenary walk into the sea after suffering a great defeat?	30
XXXVI.	Should a mercenary wish for peace?	31
XXXVII.	When should an honourable mercenary finally lay down his broadaxe?	32
XXXVIII.	Can an honourable mercenary ever find joy?	33
XXXIX.	What should be the ultimate goal of the mercenary?	34

I. What, then, is honour?

- The novice mercenary mistakes victory and wealth for honour, confusing honour with reputation. Honour is what one knows about oneself. Reputation is what others know about one.
- To be honourable, one must first understand what honour is and is not. Honour is accepting, without complaint, the burden of another's suffering because one has made himself strong enough to do so. Honour is the religion of superior men. Honour is a strength that must be developed. Yet, honour is always vulnerable. Honour that cannot be lost is not honour. However, honour is not a gift that good fortune bestows and misfortune takes back. Honour that rests on a firm foundation will not be lost through mere adversity and cannot be erased by the pyre.
- *The she bear demonstrates honour when she steps between the wolf pack and her cubs.*

II. When does a mercenary know that he is suited to his profession?

- The night before a battle, most mercenaries have broadaxe nightmares. The morning of battle, most mercenaries long to be farmers. The

evening after battle, most mercenaries see trolls gnawing of the moon.
- A mercenary knows he is suited to his profession when, during battle, after being ambushed by a dishonourable adversary, after his huscarls have deserted him, after his battle hound is dead, after he himself is mortally wounded, he is able to smile genuinely and swear: "By Odin, I would rather be nowhere else."
- *When surrounded by a dozen hounds, an ice bear is still happy to be a bear and not to be a hound.*

III. Is it possible for a Berserker to follow the path of an honourable mercenary?

- A Berserker takes pride in winning at all cost and will do anything to achieve victory.
- A mercenary has honour if he holds himself to an ideal of conduct even when it is dangerous to do so. Honour requires control and moderation. Berserkers enjoy neither.
- *A rabid dog cannot guard the camp.*

IV. Should a mercenary foreknow his adversary to be his equal?

- A novice mercenary imagines each adversary as either better or worse than himself.
- Honour is the right to demand mutual respect from an exclusive society of equals. A mercenary must always foreknow his adversary to be his equal in every way. A mercenary who believes himself either superior or inferior to his adversary is soon to join his ancestors.

- *The mercenary least confident of victory has the most reason to be confident of victory.*

V. Should a mercenary fight to redeem his honour?

- Some of the most dishonourable mercenaries win battles.
- An honourable mercenary is no more broken by failure than he is inflated by success. It is not the outcome of battle but rather the manner of conducting the battle that bestows honour. Honour cannot be lost in battle, it can only be forfeited.
- *A falcon is no less a falcon if called a chicken.*

VI. Should a mercenary boast of his battles so that he is known to the Kings?

- When a mercenary boasts, it encourages Kings to hire him in order to win more, bigger, and finer. Yet greed needs no encouragement.
- The honourable mercenary eschews titles and wealth for the sake of honour. Boasting is an unseemly attempt to manufacture courage from

cowardice. The gods and the mercenary know whether, during the battle, the mercenary's axe cut clean and his bowels held steady. What another man believes or does not believe does not make it so.
- *The ice bear's boast is a pack of dead wolves.*

VII. Does a mercenary fight for the King or for the King's cause?

- A novice mercenary questions the motives of the King and, in fear, asks whether the gods favor the King's cause.
- For an honourable mercenary it does not matter what side of the battle he is on. An honourable mercenary simply fights for the King who engages him. It is not his duty to determine the true motive of the King, the will of the King's subjects, or to determine if the King is good or bad. A mercenary does not fight for justice. Although justice is truth, truth on one island is a lie on another. Battle is infinitely simpler when motives are not ascribed to the actions of one's adversary.
- *Does a stone float because it will be used to grind wheat instead of to anchor a longboat?*

VIII. Should a mercenary accept an engagement if he believes he will be defeated?

- The novice mercenary believes the many songs extolling war that are sung by those who hope the mercenary will substitute his life for that of the King or, worse, for the King's gold.
- The honourable mercenary understands, but does not boast, that his life is no less valuable than any other man, including that of the King. The mercenary fights for the King not because the mercenary is more expendable. The mercenary

profession does not include a commitment to be death-fated.
- *The boar does not go looking for the bear.*

IX. When must a mercenary warn off his King?

- The novice mercenary often concerns himself only with the terms of his contract with his King and its benefit to the mercenary.
- Before closing the contract, as a final step, the honourable mercenary asks the King whether every effort has been made to resolve the dispute short of battle. If later the King's sons are slain and his daughters taken as spoils, this last step may well save the mercenary's life.
- *Never poke a hornet's nest when you can simply avoid the apple.*

X. If a King orders a mercenary to use subterfuge, what should be the mercenary's response?

- There will always be mercenaries who will take unfair advantage in battle and always be Kings who will hire them for that reason. The King wants only success and the spoils that success brings. The King will want a mercenary to spy, ambush, and torture as it advantages in battle. But these mercenaries and these Kings, both lacking honour, are not the men who will be spoken of in the future around the tables of the gods or the fires of their grandchildren. Such dishonourable mercenaries will live long lives made longer by the daily hell of guarding their hoards of unnecessaries.

- The honourable mercenary knows that Kings and kingdoms are fleeting and that battles and wars of Kings are as meaningless to the gods as are the disputes of ants fighting over piles of dung. So the honourable mercenary explains to the King that the mercenary is honour bound to fight the battle face to face, axe to shield, and on the field as it lies. This line may not be questioned by other mercenaries, nor by the King, nor by history.
- *The mother bear slays the hound face to face, regardless of how hungry her cubs might be.*

The Honourable Mercenary

XI. Must a mercenary always follow the instructions of his King?

- A dishonourable mercenary accepts the King's gold but rejects the King's charge.
- An honourable mercenary may not, at the same time, accept the King's gold but not follow the King's orders. Yet, above all, the honourable mercenary may follow no order that brings dishonour upon him or upon the King. It is up to

each mercenary to draw the line between blind obedience and honour. This line may not be questioned by other mercenaries, nor by the King, nor by history.

- *A good dog, so ordered, will lead his pack headlong into the mouth of a bear cave. But a good dog will not eat her puppies, no matter how hungry she gets.*

XII. Why should a King hire an honourable mercenary?

- It is true that it is a rare King who will choose honour over advantage, if given that choice.
- An honourable mercenary cannot expect any King to understand and value honour as the mercenary must. Royalty is based on blood, not honour.
- It is only by his being more skilled in battle that a King can be expected to value and engage an honourable mercenary. A warrior who is able to swim in his byrnies[1] is celebrated as the best of swimmers. Similarly, because an honourable mercenary is at a disadvantage when facing a dishonourable adversary, he must necessarily be wiser and more skilled and will appear so to the King. As a result, honour has come to be recognized as synonymous with skill and being battle-bold. An honourable mercenary must be so skilled that dishonourable tactics are simply a welcomed challenge, easily thwarted by him.
- *One never expects a pig to jump the fence when he can eat dung in his pen. But one always expects an eagle to soar, even when clutching a fish.*

---

[1] Mail armor.

XIII. Does a mercenary continue to fight for a King proven to be evil?

- The novice mercenary believes, mistakenly, that the Valkyries are always just and so they must decide all contests accordingly. The novice mercenary believes, foolishly, that the King who hired him must, for that reason alone, be both good and wise.
- The honourable mercenary knows there is both much wrong and much right in all men and in all gods and in all actions. Determining the exact proportions of right and wrong is the province of the gods and beyond the training and duties of the mercenary.
- *The dog hunts for even the vilest of masters until the dog, himself, is kicked.*

XIV. May a mercenary ever turn against his King?

- The dishonourable mercenary works for the highest bidder.
- The honourable mercenary, once engaged by a King, is but an arrow loosed by the King.
- *A mercenary, like a saex,[2] points in only one direction.*

---

2 Short sword.

XV. What is a mercenary's obligation to a King for whom he has fought?

- A novice mercenary often develops loyalty to a King once they have suffered a war together.
- A mercenary suffers a war with every King who engages him. An honourable mercenary is only attached to his honour.
- *Any attachment between the arrow and the archer makes both less effective.*

XVI. What should a mercenary charge for his services?

- The novice mercenary believes wrongly that what he does can be valued in gold. He seeks to accumulate wealth for himself as a result of the King's greed or misfortune.
- The honourable mercenary knows he can swing but one broadaxe, carry but one shield, sleep in but one bed, eat but half a goat and half satisfy but one wife. He charges the King only enough to sustain himself and his dependents through the current campaign and through the period until the next campaign. The honourable mercenary uses the scale of his life to weigh honour rather than gold.
- *The ice bear who slays the entire pack can eat only one wolf in a day.*

The Honourable Mercenary

XVII. When may a mercenary agree to share in the spoils of battle?

- Kings are infected by greed. No war has ever been started by a King who believed he had all to which he was entitled. Greed murders honour. It is impossible for a mercenary infected by greed to do battle honourably. He will spy, ambush, and torture to gain advantage.
- Kings prefer to pay a mercenary a portion of the spoils of war, which places the mercenary in the

bed of the King. But, the honourable mercenary is above Kings, elevated by his honour. A mercenary should fight for his honour. His broadaxe needs no further incentive. He should accept no compensation beyond that required to feed and equip his men and sustain his family. Only when a mercenary has nothing further to gain can he be fully available to his King and fully responsive to his honour.

- *Bears live quite well without sacks.*

XVIII. If a King promises gold for victory but does not pay his victorious mercenary, does the mercenary collect with his saex?[3]

- A dishonourable mercenary wages war for gold.
- A mercenary should never hold a King to the standards of an honourable mercenary. He does well to remember that he has been hired because of the greed or the fear of the King. An honourable mercenary who is not paid should neither slay the King nor pillage his land. But, the honourable mercenary may later accept, and indeed relish, an engagement against such King.
- *A dog will hunt whether petted or not. But a petted dog will not bite the hunter.*

---

3 Short sword.

XIX. Should a mercenary invoke the gods against his adversary?

- A mercenary flatters himself to believe he interests Odin or even Odin's horse.
- If Odin were to interrupt his leisure and assist a mercenary, it would cheapen both the mercenary's victory and his honour. The honour is in fighting on the battlefield before you with the Thanes[4] who have sworn allegiance to you. All outside advantages subtract from the honour of battle.
- *If a mercenary is known to Odin, it is but as an ant.*

XX. Should a mercenary break bread with his adversary?

- Of all the poisons of the mind, hatred is the most poisonous. Hatred always mans the rudder. A mercenary's life is in the hands of any adversary who makes him hate.
- To dishonour an adversary is to dishonour one's self. To hate an adversary is to hate one's self. It is both natural and appropriate for both animals and men of the same stripe to eat together. The King who has hired a mercenary is unlikely to understand or approve of this professional respect.

---

4 Warrior/companions.

Halfdan Oldadson

Only a bear can understand a bear. Only mercenaries can understand mercenaries. But, the King's ignorance is not a reason to act contrary to the laws of nature.
- The life of a mercenary is difficult enough without adding hatred and disrespect. To be benched at the banquet of another mercenary will increase the skill of each and make both victory and defeat more honourable.
- *An honourable mercenary knows that hatred is but hot lava that the novice mercenary holds in his hands waiting to throw on his adversary.*

XXI. Should a mercenary discuss the upcoming battle with his adversary?

- An unskilled mercenary hopes surprise will compensate for his lack of skill and courage.
- An honourable mercenary remembers that the only honourable battle is axe to shield, shield to axe. Hiding reserves, attacking in fog, or starting the battle before noon, all bring dishonour on the mercenary.
- An honourable mercenary meets with his adversary the day before battle and tells his adversary his true numbers. This may hearten or dishearten his adversary, but the numbers will not change. If a mercenary tells his numbers and, in response, his adversary lies about his own numbers, it is of no moment. The numbers were and will remain the same.
- *The ice bear is not afraid to announce his position and strength.*

XXII. Should victory be achieved through subterfuge and awful deeds if Odin favors one's cause?

- A dishonourable mercenary seeks every method to gain a favoring wind and any justification to gain an unfair advantage.

- An honourable mercenary neither spies nor ambushes nor tortures. Such tactics certainly provide advantage to the mercenary. Nevertheless, it is honour that prevents the mercenary from justifying the awful deeds that are too easy to justify during battle.
- *There is no honour in poisoning a bear. A child could do it as well as a man.*

XXIII. Can honourable mercenaries survive if dishonourable mercenaries have an advantage in battle?

- If cheating were not an advantage, the Saksen[5] would not have invented it.
- Honourable mercenaries will only disappear in one of two ways. First, they will cease to be more skilled than their adversaries and, as a result, they will die in battle. Second, they will forget or disavow the wisdom of the wisest mercenaries, will abandon their honour, and will become dishonourable mercenaries. True honour is like the leagues of black ocean under the waves. The storm has no effect on it.
- *An eagle can walk around and pick dung with the chickens, but, if he did, he would not emblazon any shields.*

---

5 Saxon.

XXIV. Should a mercenary taunt his adversary?

- A novice mercenary seeks to anger his adversary as a way of boasting and gaining an advantage in battle.
- A wise mercenary wants the battle decided with skill and courage along. He wants his adversary battle-brave with mead and skillfully swinging a sharp broadaxe.
- *When one must hunt an ice bear, there is no advantage in first angering the bear.*

XXV. How does a mercenary overcome fear?

- The novice mercenary believes that both courage and cowardice are contagious. When facing a field of weapons sparking like broken ice, he tries to summon courage by boasting, screaming and disfiguring.
- Only by knowing the true nature of fear and understanding its origin can one hope to defend against it. A mercenary never overcomes fear. An honourable mercenary simply understands that running away gets one both winded and an arrow in the arse.
- *Even the best dog shakes when he smells the ice bear. But, once loosed, he lunges for the bear's throat nonetheless.*

XXVI. Must a mercenary press the battle?

- A novice mercenary hastens to battle to curry favor with his King.
- Kings are always at war with each other because they are always at war with themselves and the gods. The battle will, invariably, come soon enough.
- *The worms get every man eventually. A pressed battle simply feeds the worms sooner.*

Halfdan Oldadson

XXVII. Should a mercenary accommodate an adversary by delaying battle?

- A dishonourable mercenary seeks to gain an advantage in battle by factors other than skill and courage.
- Victory is only honourable when it is the best at their best fighting the best.
- *The hunter's family does not sing of his slaying an old bear caught in a trap.*

XXVIII. Is there a way to best engage a dishonourable adversary?

- The novice mercenary concerns himself with the honour or lack of honour of his adversary.
- An honourable mercenary fights best when he does not ascribe motives to the actions of his adversary. Once loosed, the power of an arrow to pierce the byrnies[6] does not depend on the wishes of the archer.
- Only with warriors in battle, with lawspeakers in the Althing, and with athletes in their contests do men, equally skilled, attempt to thwart every action of one another. Yet, this is the quintessence of the profession the mercenary has chosen. Better to consider battles as an athletic contest than as a fight to the death. The outcome will be the same, but you will not be distracted by the motives of your adversary.
- *It makes no difference whether the bear you hunt seeks to embarrass you or is merely hungry. Once the bear attacks, you must parry his blows nonetheless.*

XXIX. How does a mercenary treat the uninvolved?

---

[6] Mail armor.

- The novice mercenary allays his fears and simplifies his task by treating even the uninvolved as adversaries.
- The honourable mercenary takes care to spare the uninvolved. There is no honour in slaying those who are not equally capable of slaying you. An honourable mercenary obeys the Law of the Innocents.[7]
- *The fisherman returns to the sea the fish he cannot eat, even though this requires additional effort.*

XXX. Are there some throats that should not feel the saex?[8]

- Once the tide of battle has turned, it is easy to spare no adversary. Honour in battle is always easier than honour in victory. Honour is tested most when a mercenary has the freedom to do as he wishes.
- Always show mercy but never grovel for it yourself. An honourable mercenary spares everyone he is able. There is no honour in slaying one more warrior or burning one more home if it will not decide the battle. An honourable mercenary is careful always to spare those forced into battle for they are unlikely to return to fight against him.
- *The ice bear finds no honour in eating carrion.*

---

[7] A.D. 697 law written by Abbot of Iona protecting non-combatants.
[8] Short sword.

XXXI. Is a mercenary responsible for the acts of his huscarls?[9]

- A dishonourable mercenary blames his huscarls for defeat yet takes all the acclaim for victory.
- As the Berzerkers say, of the sixty huscarls who fill a longboat, fifty are mere targets, nine are true warriors, but only one can bring the longboat home.
- *The archer is responsible for the path of the arrow.*

---
9 Troops.

XXXII. Once victorious, should a mercenary disfigure his adversary?

- Disfiguring is the worst boasting.
- A cruel act is no less condemnable when it is committed in battle than when it is committed in one's home. Remember that a mercenary can take arms and legs but cannot take honour.
- *An honourable mercenary clears the path for his adversary's retreat.*

XXXIII. If a mercenary fights for an evil King, is he more likely to die?

- The novice mercenary believes foolishly that the King's reputation can influence the outcome of the battle.
- The gods do not pronounce a King good or bad, so a mercenary will never know for which he fights. The mercenary should concentrate on what he can command: his preparation, his plan of attack, his battle skills and, above all, his honour.
- *Does it matter to the wolf mother if she fights for her grey cub or her brown cub?*

XXXIV. When must a mercenary surrender?

- A novice mercenary surrenders based on his misunderstanding that surviving to fight again is the equivalent of fighting well.
- An honourable mercenary always maintains his courage. When faced with a fearful situation, he asks himself, whether it is truly dire or whether it is simply that more effort is needed. It is almost always the latter.
- When things are truly dire, the best advice comes from the Berserkers' song: When things are

hopeless, there is only one hope - to fight like there is no hope.

- *Until the ice bear sees his own arse being dragged into the woods by the hounds, he believes the hounds cannot defeat him. Yet, that is the very moment when the ice bear doubles his efforts.*

XXXV. Should a mercenary walk into the sea after suffering a great defeat?

- A mercenary flatters himself when he believes it was he who won or lost a battle.

- Slaying oneself is the ultimate boast. A mercenary is given a field, weapons, warriors and, if he is lucky, allies in Valhalla, each of which may be better or worse than those of his adversary. An honourable mercenary is humble so that he understands that all he can provide is his maximum effort.
- *Take neither the glory of victory nor the ignominy of defeat. A battle does not decide who is just or whom the gods favor or who is honourable. The only thing a battle decides is whom the worms will eat today and whom the worms will eat tomorrow.*

XXXVI. Should a mercenary wish for peace?

- A mercenary flatters himself to think his wishing can change anything.
- An honourable mercenary knows that his wishes hold no power. There will always be Kings and kingdoms full of abject subjects. Each King wants more than the next King and wants more so badly that he will happily sacrifice everything his subjects have to obtain it.
- *Fighting to stop fighting is as futile as eating to stop eating.*

XXXVII. When should an honourable mercenary finally lay down his broadaxe?

- Each time the svinfylking[10] approaches, the mercenary, like the oak, gains another ring.
- Through skill, years of battle, and discipline a novice mercenary becomes an honourable mercenary. Thereafter, he can no more retire than a wolf can cease to be a wolf or a chicken cease to

---

10 Flying wedge.

be a chicken. His battles may become fewer and less important, but he must fight until he reaches Valhalla.
- *Even the oldest eagle does not climb down from his nest.*

XXXVIII. Can an honourable mercenary ever find joy?

- There is one truth common to all men who are not mercenaries: they spend their lives seeking freedom from pain.
- All are born to pain. An honourable mercenary does not avoid pain. He assumes the pain of another for a price. That is his profession. Pain is how a mercenary knows he is alive. Pain is how a mercenary measures his effort. Only the dead know no pain.
- Happiness is impossible for a mercenary because, for him to be truly effective, he must always both anticipate the worst and bear the pain that would otherwise be that of the King. That is his profession. The mercenary substitutes honour for happiness.
- *The eagle never smiles.*

XXXIX. What should be the ultimate goal of the mercenary?

- The misguided mercenary comes to believe that he is responsible for his victories and that his successes impress the gods. He hopes, foolishly, to take gold with him to Valhalla.
- Yet, the mercenary cannot control the tide of battle any more than a fish can control the tides. A battle may turn on a single oar broken by the Valkyries at the hidden knot formed long before the mercenary was born. All the mercenary can control are his own actions and his own honour. In the end, his actions disappear with the past and all he has is his honour and his family.
- *The ultimate goal of every mercenary is to teach his grandson to laugh heartily and his granddaughter to sing often. If he waged war as an honourable mercenary, then, perhaps his grandchildren will laugh heartily and sing often in remembrance of him.*

The Honourable Mercenary

www.ingramcontent.com/pod-product-compliance
Lightning Source LLC
Chambersburg PA
CBHW072313200526
45168CB00014B/1421